Up, up and Away

Hello!

NORTH YORKSHIRE

Edited by Dave Thomas

First published in Great Britain in 2000 by
YOUNG WRITERS
Remus House,
Coltsfoot Drive,
Peterborough, PE2 9JX
Telephone (01733) 890066

HB ISBN 075432 114 2
SB ISBN 075432 115 0

FOREWORD

This year, the Young Writers' Up, Up & Away competition proudly presents a showcase of the best poetic talent from over 70,000 up-and-coming writers nationwide.

Successful in continuing our aim of promoting writing and creativity in children, our regional anthologies give a vivid insight into the thoughts, emotions and experiences of today's younger generation, displaying their inventive writing in its originality.

The thought, effort, imagination and hard work put into each poem impressed us all and again the task of editing proved challenging due to the quality of entries received, but was nevertheless enjoyable. We hope you are as pleased as we are with the final selection and that you continue to enjoy *Up, Up & Away North Yorkshire* for many years to come.

CONTENTS

Baldersby St James CE School

Caitlin Rushby	18
Emily Roy	19
Katie Cairns	19
James Mollard	20
Rebecca Ogden	20
Conor Rushby	21
Jamie Smith	21
Eleanor Hawkesworth	22
Anna Kettlewell	22
Dannielle Smith	23
Jonathan Branscombe	23
Hannah Ogden	23
Callum Scott	24
Jodie Smith	24
Sam Knox	25

Bilsdale Midcable Chop Gate CE School

Sarah Cook	25
Martin Cook	26
David Jackson	26
Robert Wilson	26
Emma Fulcher	27
Sarah Johnson	27
William Forbes	27
Amelia Easton	28
Tamsin Macdonald	28
Tom Fulcher	29
Tracey Johnson	29
Kelly Brown	30
Tiffany Smith	30
Elizabeth Stanton	30
David Gerrard	31

Colburn CP School

Dean Bowes	31
Nichola Collinson	32
Kayleigh Wilcox	32

Kimberley Pattison	49
Josh Cripps	49
Elizabeth Richardson	50
Steven Nix	50
Lee Emmerson	51
Emily Palmer	52
Alice Leake	52
Hayley Bell	53
Shelley Hobson	53
Daniel Kneen	54
Luke Ryans	54
Kirsty Mycoe	55
Jane Bond	55
Abigail Jones	56
Lucy Whitehead	56
Luke Roberts	57
Gareth Thirlwell	57
Gemma Greener	58
Alice Gibbs	59

Horton in Ribblesdale CE Primary School

Hope Boscock	59
Karen Lambert	60
Ethan Boocock	60
Beth Algie	61
Holly Connaughton	62
Matthew Holgate	62
Katie Fox	63
Jessie Alston	63
Becky Wilcock	64
Steven Millman	64

Kettlewell School

Bianca Briggs	65
Edward Hird	65
Hannah Locker	65
Iona Wood-Katic	66
Tiffany Briggs	66

Andrew Mallinson	66
Iain Howarth	67
Amie Locker	67
Emily Rackham	67
Philippa Mallinson	68
Simon Johnston	68
Harriet Rackham	69
James Middleton	69
David Hird	70
Harvey Briggs	70

Knayton CE Primary School

Sarah Hill	71
Robin Cook	71
Sam Looker	72
Matthew Wingrove	72
Jessica Jenyns	73
Stephanie Christon	73
Olivia Bentley	74
Sarah Coidan	74
Rosalyn Mogridge	75
Laura Keast	76
Lorna Spence	77
Tom Harrison	77
Oliver Morgan-Williams	78
Gavin Lovell	78
John Tough	79
Laura Roberts	79
Kate Ward	80
Charlotte Muxlow	81

Langcliffe County Primary School

Sophie Meredith	82
Andrew Jeffrey	82

Le Cateau Primary School

Nadine Milligan & Oriana Smith	83
George Curtis	84

Emily Marshall	84
Michelle Allen	85
Scott McGuffie	86
Kimberley Gray	86
Oriana Smith	87
Fiona Hunt	88
Lloyd Parker	88
Josephine Keating	89
Sarah Cohen	89
Carley Evers	90
James Murray	90
Kirsty Graham-Battersby	91
William Gillan	91
Sarah Williams	92
Lauren Smart	92
Andrew Robson	93
George Curtis	94
Marianne Best	94

Roecliffe CE Primary School

Jamie Gareth Lewis	95
Hollie Bramley	96
Ben Wilson	97

St Mary's RC School, Malton

Henry Whittington	97
Stephanie Johnson	98
Sean Quinn	98
Natalie Rookes	99
Elizabeth Harvey	100

Snape County Primary School

Danielle Graham	100
Rebecca Djoric	101
James Deal	101
Charlotte Deal	102
Imogen Brown	102
David Sharpe	103

The Poems

THE MILLENNIUM BUG

T   he Bug is here!
H   elp is needed
E   veryone watch out!

M   idnight of Friday 31st,
I   t's going to come out.
L   ots of munching,
L   ots of crunching,
E   asy to sort.
N   o!
N   ot at all!
I   t's going to eat your chips,
U   psetting your computer
M   any Bugs do their work!

B   e organised,
U   ntil the year 2000,
G   *et it sorted!*

Emma Bolton (9)

TEACHERS

In a way teachers are helpful in the playground.
They are referees and they cure people's knees
And they help you when you are playing around.

In a way teachers are very helpful in the classroom.
They try and get you a good education
And when you're older you might just get a good occupation.

Emma-Lee Orton (10)
Airy Hill CP School

TELEVISION

Why do we watch television?
I'd rather do nuclear fission.
It's only some junk, for really bad punks.
So why do we watch television?

> Why do we watch the box?
> I'd rather eat smelly socks.
> Television's not cool, so why does it rule?
> Why do we watch the box?

But I ask myself this question,
It may be a silly suggestion.
So stop watching Noo-Noo when there's plenty to do.
Now turn off the box right away!

David Fester (9)
Airy Hill CP School

MY CAT

My cat is very fat
She will sleep anywhere
Up above or down below
She will sleep anywhere
She will eat fish
Big or small
She wouldn't care less
My cat jumps up at me
When I come in from school.

Normally when I go to bed
She comes up too
Just to say goodnight
But she normally gives me a fright.

Amber Whisson (9)
Airy Hill CP School

THE DOLL

My sister has a plastic doll,
She thinks that it's a winner,
She plays with it all day long
And feeds it Sunday dinner.

I wish, if I only could,
Just get it for this once,
I'd throw and spin it round and round,
Then I'd try to bin it.

I don't think it will work though,
I've tried it before.
She cries and cries and cries and cries,
And cries a little more.

She grabs the doll straight from my hand
And storms off to her room.
A couple of minutes later,
She's behind me with a broom . . .
Ow!
                    She'll see, that doll's out of here!

Jessica Keys (11)
Airy Hill CP School

THE SOUNDS IN THE PLAYGROUND

What can I hear in the playground?
The wind blowing wild
And the screaming of a child.
The sound of the footballers
Cheering when they score,
The knocking and the slamming
Of the junior door.

The girls singing a song
When they are skipping
And the wailing of a girl
When someone's been nipping.

The infants dancing the Conga
And doing their wailing
But there's always one, just one
Who's always complaining.

So do you really like the sounds
In the playground?
Well I know I'd prefer it
If there was no sound.

Kelly Hogarth (11)
Airy Hill CP School

SHOES

I'm going to the shoe shop,
It's going to be fun today.
I'm trying all the shoes on,
Each one a different way.

I've already got some shoes,
So I don't really care.
I'm always comfortable,
No matter what I wear.

There's trainers and flip-flops and wellies,
And sandals that sometimes are jellies.
Some of the ladies wear high heels,
And crazy people wear orange peels.

I like the shoes I wear each day,
I wouldn't change them in any way.

Sarah Crossan (9)
Airy Hill CP School

MATHS

Add, take away, times and divide
I'd rather run away and hide
All this hard maths to do
I like art best, don't you?

I'll probably be here all night
And I'll fight my teacher
Fight, fight, and fight.

All this hard maths to do
I'll be here till half-past two
When all the owls go *tu-whit tu-whoo*
All this hard maths to do
Oh look, art - that doesn't make me sick
But in a few months I probably won't like it.

Katie Swales (9)
Airy Hill CP School

MY MUM AND DAD

My mum and dad are always saying,
'Do this, do that,'
I'd like to hit them with a baseball bat.
My mum looks after three wailing babies,
She just isn't a proper lady.
My dad drives all day in his noisy truck,
I think I'd rather read a book.

I think our house is rather small,
My friend's house is extremely tall.
When my dad is off work, he is very lazy,
And my mum is going rather crazy.
My dad and brother are mad about football,
It drives my mum and I up the wall.

My mum and dad at the moment are very mad with me,
They won't even let me invite one single friend round for tea.
My mum and dad are trying to diet,
Maybe for once it will keep them quiet.
I only have one mum and dad,
And between you and me, I love them like mad!

Hannah Wardell (10)
Airy Hill CP School

ELEPHANTS

The elephant is a hungry beast,
He likes to eat and make a feast.
His footprints dig in the sand and
Are seen throughout the land.
The sound of his trunk
Is louder than the lion's roar
And greater than the cutting saw.

Scott Grason (10)
Airy Hill CP School

Cats

Cats in the garden
Cats in the house
Cats in the garage
Eating a mouse
Cats are cute
Cats are wise
Cats are good at catching flies
Cats can play
Cats can sleep
Cats like lots of things to eat
Cats are cruel
Cats are sly
Cats can climb really high
But when they want to go to sleep
They curl up tight and look so sweet.

Laura Hewitt (10)
Airy Hill CP School

Football Champion

The fans get on their chairs
Before the match begins,
The crowd goes crazy
Hoping their team will win.
The whistle blows, the game starts
They get the ball and score one goal,
They did it ten more times.
The whistle goes again
The team on the left side scored one goal.
Then they get on the pitch
They were bored so they acted wild.
The match was over, the score was *11-1!*

Graham Miller (8)
Airy Hill CP School

HOMEWORK

Homework, homework, it's not fair.
Teachers, teachers, just don't care.
All the kids are in agony.
All the kids agree with me.

But please don't argue,
Please don't fight,
There's only one thing to say -
I hate homework.

Technology, maths, anything to do with homework,
All the kids hate it.
We'd rather live in a pit.

But please don't argue, please don't fight,
There's only one thing to say -
I hate homework.

Ashley Davies (9)
Airy Hill CP School

MOTORCROSS

Dreading the jumps ahead
Tabletops and all kinds
Turning round in the air,
Breaking records everywhere
Breaking bones down below
Lots of mud on their clothes
Relatives bellow, *'Go, go, go.'*

Bill Orrell (9)
Airy Hill CP School

IF I COULD HAVE AN ANIMAL

If I could have an animal,
I wonder what I'd have?
I could choose a big fierce lion
To eat up Mrs Crabb,
Or I could have a lovely bird
To keep as my pet.
Or I could have butterflies
And catch them in a net,
I could even have a crocodile
And call him Mr Smith.
I might only have a little cat,
Or a colourful fish.
I could have a furry bear,
Or a rat, or mouse,
Or even an elephant
And keep it in my house.
I would love a tiger,
With stripes all down his back,
Or a prickly hedgehog,
Or snakes in a sack.
Puppies are adorable,
So are little ducks,
And leopards with their black spots,
Or hens that go *cluck.*
But the thing that really upsets me,
The thing that makes me sad,
Is Mum is allergic to animals,
(I find that really bad.)

Rebecca Swales (9)
Airy Hill CP School

GARRY GADGET

Garry Gadget spends his days
in his smelly shed,
banging, sawing, drilling, clanging,
hardly goes to bed.
In the morning, 6 o'clock,
he will be outside,
banging, sawing, drilling, clanging,
till the day he dies.
Housewife robots, sweet machines,
anything he wants,
banging, sawing, drilling, clanging,
will he ever stop?
But surely, this tireless boy,
will one day break down and . . . *pop!*

Samuel Winter (10)
Airy Hill CP School

MORE MATHS

Why do we always have more maths,
I'd rather have a thousand baths,
We never stop doing maths, maths, maths,
But I'd never fly an aircraft.

Do you like maths? Well I don't,
I'd rather have a new coat,
Maths after maths after maths too,
One of the kids said 'I hate you!'

Doing my maths is boring,
I'd rather hear my dad snoring,
But I still hate maths,
I hate maths!

Rachel Allan (9)
Airy Hill CP School

HARRY THE HAMSTER

My pet hamster is called Harry.
He does not eat normal hamster food.
When we clean him out,
He runs down the stairs and gets some food
Like jelly, toast, chips, even pizza.
My hamster Harry might be greedy
But we still like him,
Even if he eats all of our sandwiches.
He runs in his wheel all day and night,
It gives us a fright
When we see him eating crisps, beans, even eggs,
Mum goes downstairs,
She looks in the fridge, there is no food.
In his bed there is loads of food
But I still love my hamster Harry.

Laura Purves (8)
Airy Hill CP School

WHAT WOULD I DO?

What would I do if my ears were blue,
And my nose was pink and as big as a sink,
And my eyes were white and as big as a kite,
Oh what would I do?

Oh what would I do if my mouth was small and I was tall,
My fingers were green and I was mean,
My toes were brown, each wearing a crown,
Oh what would I do?

And what would I do if my arms were gold and I was cold,
My nails were torn and my hair was shorn,
And what would I do if you were not you,
Oh what would I do?

Jamie-Lee Bain (9)
Airy Hill CP School

POLLY

My dog Polly eats anything,
Brussel sprouts, turkey, puddings,
Cereals, milk, bacon, eggs, toast,
Potatoes, mash, carrots, peas and Sunday roast.
Sandwiches, crisps and jelly,
She even likes chewing my dad's wellie.
Sausages big and small,
Vegetables and that's not all.
Toad in the hole, beans and ham,
Anything but *my mam*.
But . . .
I love my Polly.

Beth Grason (8)
Airy Hill CP School

MY BEST FRIEND

Shannon is my best friend
She'll be my friend till the very end
We play together all day long
And then at night we sing a song.
Sometimes we play at home together
In all sorts of different weather
If it's wet we play inside
At a game called seek and hide.
If the weather's nice and warm
We go and watch the bees all swarm.
Sometimes we fall out
But without a doubt
We get back together
As friends forever.

Hannah Brown (10)
Airy Hill CP School

DOGS

Big dogs, small dogs,
Yappy and naughty dogs,
Some lick, some bite,
Shaggy and raggy dogs,
Soft and furry dogs,
Guzzling food all day long,
Then after that their hunger's gone,
Racing around on the grass,
Chasing butterflies, mice and trash,
After that they are tired,
So they go to sleep next to the fire.

Kayleigh Taylor (8)
Airy Hill CP School

MY CAT

My cat is fat.
He sleeps on a mat.
His name is William.
He is black and white and furry.
He's not allowed out at night
Because he has only got one eye.
If you want to know why,
He went to the vet,
He's only got one eye.

Georgia Keys (8)
Airy Hill CP School

THE RUN

Oh no, the trial today,
It's the big race on Monday.
I told my mum I had wobbly feelings in my tum
And that my heart was beating like a drum.
Some were slow and one had a broken toe,
But deep down below, I knew I would put on a good show
And win the race.

Robbie Unsworth (9)
Airy Hill CP School

THE VULGAR FRENCHMAN FROM FRANCE

There was once a vulgar Frenchman from France
Who often put ants down his pants
But when there's an itch, he starts to twitch
That vulgar Frenchman from France.

Simon Hankin (10)
Airy Hill CP School

MY DOG

Do you want to know
My dog Bruno?

Do you want to know?
I will tell you so.

Bruno is brown and white,
Some people think
He is a fright.

But I think he is alright.

Abigail Orton (8)
Airy Hill CP School

MY CAT

My cat died.
A car ran over him.
I cried
Because he died.
I wish he would come back.
I love my cat.

Adam Poole (8)
Airy Hill CP School

MY FRIEND POLLY

My friend Polly,
Loves her dolly,
Every day she runs away
And her friends think she's a wally.
She's extremely tall,
She drives me up the wall,
She loves cats
And adores rats,
And owns an orange ball.

Emma Harland (10)
Airy Hill CP School

CATS AND DOGS

Cats and dogs
Always fight
You never know who is who
They run so fast
They might never stop
But if they do
They'll start again
In a bit, you just watch.

Emma Hall (10)
Airy Hill CP School

IN THE BATHROOM

In the bathroom,
Scrub, scrub, scrub,
I'm washing my hair,
Rub, rub, rub.

Playing in the bath,
Fight, fight, fight,
With my sister,
Every night.

Getting the soap,
Oops! Gone down the drain,
Put my finger down,
Got stuck again.

Got out of the bath,
Dried my hair,
Got ready for bed
And cuddled my bear.

I cuddle up in bed,
Every night,
Mum comes in,
I say goodnight.

Up early in the morning,
Ready for school,
Travelling there,
We play the fool.

Rebecca Gibson (10)
Airy Hill CP School

MY DAD

My dad is so silly,
He makes me laugh.
I never stop laughing.
When my mum says
'Go to the shop,' he just whines.
My mum has to pay him.
But I still love him,
Well, he isn't bad.

Joseph Blacklock (8)
Airy Hill CP School

ELEPHANT

The creased elephant moves across the wild African plain,
Reaching for the dry grass,
Entwining the once green shoots with his powerful trunk,
Like a boa constrictor,
Curling, squeezing, some innocent creature.

A rustle in the grasses brings the elephant back to reality,
The shiny barrel of a gun visible through the undergrowth.
He rears. The hunter, in alarm, scrambles away.
The elephant trumpets through his mighty trunk.
The elephant knows what he came for.
Elephants never forget.

Night descends on the plain.
The calls of birds echo in the grasslands.
Above, the African stars twinkle,
They know what has happened.
They watch silently during the day,
At night they reveal their true beauty.

Caitlin Rushby (10)
Baldersby St James CE School

CATS

Cats can be as smooth as silk or as rough as a cord carpet.
You can never be exactly sure of what a cat is thinking.
They can be as sudden as a flash of lightning
Or as slow as an old tortoise.
They can be happy or sad,
Good or bad.
This mysterious behaviour makes them the purr. . .fect mousetrap.
Suddenly a mouse crosses the large plain.
The cat creeps like a lion stalking a zebra
In the heat of the Savannah sun.
Then sprinting like an athlete, it runs and pounces.
The mouse draws its last breath,
The cat the victor.

Emily Roy (10)
Baldersby St James CE School

LIVERPOOL FC

I wish I had more money
so that I could go to see
Liverpool Football Club play
more often than I do now.
(They could become the greatest team in history
all because of me.)

I wish I had more money,
I know it can't buy everything like love and war,
but please give me ten quid,
just to see Liverpool once more.

Katie Cairns (11)
Baldersby St James CE School

Do You Like?

Do you like sticky treacle tart?
Do you like wobbly orange jelly?
Do you like cold fresh milk?
I do, do you?

Do you like chocolate ice-cream?
Do you like warm apple pie?
Do you like grilled bacon sandwiches?
I do, do you?

Do you like green Brussel sprouts?
Do you like red squashy tomatoes?
Do you like soggy, watery cabbage?
Yuk! I don't, do you?

James Mollard (9)
Baldersby St James CE School

All About Horses

Hay-muncher
        apple-cruncher
hoof-stomper
        carrot-chomper
water-drinker
        funny-winker
mud-roller
        cloth-holer.

Rebecca Ogden (10)
Baldersby St James CE School

THE WOLF

Slowly, slowly creeping, he pounces,
But the prey gets away.
Sparkling eyes turn to the winter sun,
The beast's mouth watering.
Then a rabbit runs past, teeth sink into the red flesh.
At last the King has his meal.

Sitting on his rock, he watches his sleeping kingdom
And lets out a bloodcurdling howl.
He trots to his home -
A hollow tree, bones on the floor.
Lying on a bed of moss,
The wolf begins his endless sleep.

Conor Rushby (8)
Baldersby St James CE School

LOVE AND HATE

Love is romance like Mum and Dad
Love is friends like Ross and I
Love is grandparents like me and Grandad
Love is computers like Ross and the PlayStation.

Hate is brother and sister like Dannielle and I
Hate is war like the Blitz
Hate is just stupid but it can't be helped.

I'd rather be loved than hated.

Jamie Smith (11)
Baldersby St James CE School

HORSES

If I had a horse . . .

I would have a dapple grey.
It would be as grey as a raincloud.

Or, I might have a black horse.
It would be as black as the night sky.

Or, I may choose a ginger one,
The colour of a crunchy biscuit.

Don't worry, you can please me
With any horse.

Eleanor Hawkesworth (7)
Baldersby St James CE School

FEELINGS

When I feel happy I smile and laugh
When I feel sad I cry and frown
When I feel angry I scream and shout
When I feel excited I jump up and down
When I feel tired I yawn and shut my eyes
When I feel lonely I sit and sulk
When I feel cross I stamp my feet.
        Feelings are me.

Anna Kettlewell (9)
Baldersby St James CE School

BROTHERS

B ossy
R aving
O bstinate
T errible
H ideous
E vil
R evolting
S illy . . . brothers.

Dannielle Smith (9)
Baldersby St James CE School

SHARKS

S harp teeth
H ard-skinned
A ngry-minded
R ed-toothed
K illing jaws
S harp-finned.

Jonathan Branscombe (9)
Baldersby St James CE School

MY DIARY

My diary is full of truth and mistakes.
It has lots of love birds, lots of secrets.
My diary has lots of things I do every day,
Just little notes or even long things to say.
It's full of secrets, good things and bad.
It's for my eyes only!

Hannah Ogden (8)
Baldersby St James CE School

GIRLFRIEND

G rand
I ntelligent
R oses
L ikeable
F riendly
R adiant
I nseparable
E legant
N ice
D elightful.

Callum Scott (8)
Baldersby St James CE School

BOYFRIEND

B eautiful
O bedient
Y oung
F antastic
R adiant
I ntelligent
E xcellent
N ice
D rop-dead gorgeous.

Jodie Smith (7)
Baldersby St James CE School

CATS

Soft fur
Big hunter
Spiky ears
Loud miaower
Big snuggler
Good fighter
Fancy runner
Wet nose
Scary cat
Big explorer
Brilliant stripes
That's my cat.

Sam Knox (7)
Baldersby St James CE School

THE LISTENERS

He walked alone,
Quietly to the door;
He turned, and then
He looked in at the empty room,
Beyond the foggy window
But there was only the ghost of . . .
                    his long lost love.

He had searched for centuries,
But no one had seen
Or heard his silent search,
I listened to his distraught cries
Then I sat back and sighed,
I was distraught to reach him
But dare I really?

Sarah Cook (11)
Bilsdale Midcable Chop Gate CE School

ANGER

Anger is purple like bruises,
It tastes like wiggly worms,
It smells like wasted petrol,
Fork lightning piercing the skies,
It sounds like the roar of an angry lion,
And the feeling is like being boiled in a kettle.
Boiling!

Martin Cook (9)
Bilsdale Midcable Chop Gate CE School

LOVE

Red like sweet roses
Love tastes like melted chocolate
Love smells like strawberries and sugar
Love looks like newborn puppies
Love sounds like sparrows singing away in the trees
Love feels soft and weak.

David Jackson (10)
Bilsdale Midcable Chop Gate CE School

LOVE

Love is as red as a rose and as sweet as pineapple pie.
Love smells like harvest time when the bales are just being made.
Love looks like a rose petal just falling to the ground.
Love sounds like the shouts of happiness.
Love makes me feel safe.

Robert Wilson (9)
Bilsdale Midcable Chop Gate CE School

LOVE

The colour of love is pink
The taste of love is strawberry ice-cream, it makes me blink
The smell of love is perfume, it will always make me think of
                                    lollipops and lemonade drinks
The sound of love is laughing like a baby gurgling
Love makes me feel like my mum's arms are around me.

Emma Fulcher (8)
Bilsdale Midcable Chop Gate CE School

WICKEDNESS

Wickedness is dark green
It tastes like the fire of Hell
The smell is like smoke
It looks like the Devil
The sound is crackling in my ears
It feels like the pain in the bottom
                            of your heart.

Sarah Johnson (10)
Bilsdale Midcable Chop Gate CE School

JEALOUSY

Jealousy is envy with green edges.
Jealousy tastes like raw meat, cold beans and old gravy.
Jealousy smells like a sewage line.
Jealousy looks like a crowded, smelly and littered old city.
Jealousy sounds like a monster stamping down a dark street.
Jealousy feels like rough, dead skin and sharp knives against my hand.

William Forbes (10)
Bilsdale Midcable Chop Gate CE School

AUTUMN POEM

Cold autumn wind blowing through leaves,
The helicopters fly through the sky,
Conkers fall everywhere.

Cold autumn days blowing my hair,
Pea pods bursting everywhere,
Berries on the rowan tree,
Blackbirds eat them all for tea.

Cold autumn months passing by day by day,
Children picking conkers all the time,
Not many helicopters flying around now,
Autumn is coming to an end.

Amelia Easton (10)
Bilsdale Midcable Chop Gate CE School

HATE

Hate
Is red to me,
It tastes like worms,
It smells like a grazed knee,
It looks like a squashed snail on your path,
It sounds like my teacher scraping her hands
                                    down the board.
Hate makes me feel very down in the dumps.

Tamsin Macdonald (10)
Bilsdale Midcable Chop Gate CE School

APPLE

Luscious and lots of
Speckly greens all over
Smooth, velvety and soft
Sweet extravagant odours
Crunchy and very crackly
Juicy, sweet, sour and sherbety
Soft, sweet and sour
Gorgeous and excellent
Sour, scrumptious apple
With sweet parts everywhere
Gone!

Tom Fulcher (11)
Bilsdale Midcable Chop Gate CE School

HATE

Hate is black.
Hate makes me mad.
The taste makes me sick.
The smell makes me go mad and dizzy.
I look like a bull with red eyes.
The sound feels like a high-pitched noise.
It makes me shaky.

Tracey Johnson (10)
Bilsdale Midcable Chop Gate CE School

LOVE

Red is the colour of love,
It tastes like a strawberry ice-cream on a Sunday afternoon,
It smells like a cream and raspberry pudding,
It looks vibrant, a bumpy, bumbly oval shape,
It sounds like a droplet of water dropping on the floor,
It makes me feel soft and weak.

Kelly Brown (11)
Bilsdale Midcable Chop Gate CE School

HAPPINESS

Happiness tastes like Ready Brek,
Happiness smells like pink ice-cream,
Happiness looks like our Buster running across the field,
Happiness sounds like a piano playing in my head,
Happiness feels like being at school.

Tiffany Smith (9)
Bilsdale Midcable Chop Gate CE School

SHYNESS

Shyness tastes like coleslaw
Shyness smells like the quickest sniff at flowers
Shyness looks like someone hiding behind their hands
Shyness sounds like someone squealing
Shyness feels like a prickly jumper being washed.

Elizabeth Stanton (7)
Bilsdale Midcable Chop Gate CE School

CURIOSITY

Curiosity is a murky blue hanging in your brain.
It hangs like the taste of something you don't like.
Curiosity smells like fish fingers cooking,
A hand creeping round a wall.
Curiosity sounds like a drum beating in your head.
It feels like desperation - you've got to know.

David Gerrard (9)
Bilsdale Midcable Chop Gate CE School

SEASONS

Spring is the beginning
The seed
A baby
Blue and green.

Summer is a holiday
The flowering
A child
Yellow and blue.

Autumn is giving up
The withering
An adult
Brown and gold.

Winter is the end
The death
An elderly
White and black.

Spring is a new life.

Dean Bowes (10)
Colburn CP School

A COLOUR POEM

Yellow is the colour of the sun.
Yellow is a bright colour that has been done.
Yellow is a happy colour, not sad.
Yellow makes you smile like mad.
Yellow is the colour of the sand.
Yellow is the colour of your hairband.

Red is a spicy chilli.
Red is a Bonfire Night.
Red is a colour of a bright light.
Red is a colour when you are sick of your sister.
Red is a sizzling blister.

Blue is a deep blue sea.
Blue is a colour when you are freezing in winter just like me.
Blue is a bluebell.
Blue is a colour when you are not very well.
Blue is a colour of the water.
Blue is the colour of a quarter.
Blue is the colour when you are sad.
Blue is the colour when you are very mad.

Nichola Collinson (11)
Colburn CP School

PLAYTIMES

Yo-yos bouncing
Bullies pouncing
Screaming, shouting
Party people racing
Marbles rolling
Teachers yawning
Cops and robbers, people are falling
Someone in a corner
Giving out an order.

Ring, ring, ring goes the bell
Children are lining up very well
When the bell goes again
Kiddies are saying 'Yeah'
A child from the corner is asked to play
If he says yes he'll have a good day.

Kayleigh Wilcox (11)
Colburn CP School

FRIDAY'S FLOOD!

I was in the toilet on Friday,
trying to wash my hands.
Suddenly the pipes split open
and started to expand.

I hurried to the staff room
and started banging on the door.
'Come quickly' Miss Riley,
'There's lots of water on the floor.'

She clambered down the stairway
and hurried for the mop.
'I'm telling you Miss Riley,
It just kind of . . . popped!'

'Oh come on dear, just shut that mouth,
We need to get the plumber out.
Just ring them now,
Just ring them quick,
No need to worry, he'll have it fixed.'

Ashleigh Reid (11)
Colburn CP School

TODAY I FEEL

I'll explode with joy and laughter,
I'll sing to the birds on a cool day,
I'll jump with happiness and freedom
On the playground.
Why? 'Cause I feel happy.

I'll collapse in the corner,
I'll fall downstairs,
I'll even squash a fly,
Why? 'Cause I feel unhappy.

Today I feel like a cold, rough breeze,
Like a ball of goo,
Like a big pain,
Why? 'Cause I feel ill.

Today I feel like a big red bubble,
Like the word 'rage',
Like a selfish child,
Why? 'Cause I feel angry.

Brigette Martin (11)
Colburn CP School

AN EVIL WITCH

The wind is an angry witch,
Raging over something nobody knows.

She smashes,
She bashes,
She tears,
She crumbles.

A storm is brewing,
Add some evil and a couple of rumbles.
The sun comes out and fights the wind.
She dies and a rainbow comes out
To show she is beaten.

Alistair Kirkby (10)
Colburn CP School

THE RAGING SEA

Someone has angered the mighty sea,
And now the sinner has to pay,
For they have killed his favourite whale.
The price this man now has to shed
Is something all mankind should dread.

Oh how he rages looking for thee,
Killing anybody in his way.
He wrecks every vessel,
He swamps the land
And with one spit, my boat he strands.

Soon we start to pine for food,
For we do not dare go out to sea,
For fear we'll never come back again.
So we can catch no more fish,
But mighty sea, who you want is me.

Kirsty Worboys (10)
Colburn CP School

ORANGE

Orange is the sunset rising in the sky,
Orange is the face of a person smiling,
Orange is the pumpkin - lighting up his face,
Orange is the moon lighting up in space,
Orange is the fire keeping us warm,
Orange is the joy when a new baby's born,
Orange is a shadow of the water when it's dark,
Orange can sometimes make us feel sad,
Orange is the tiger creeping through the grass,
Orange is the bear hunting its prey,
Orange is the woman sleeping away,
Orange is a baby when it's crying,
Orange is the feeling when someone's dying.

Lindsay McClean (11)
Colburn CP School

DOGS

There's hyperactive dogs who won't stay still
And lazy dogs who won't move at all.

There's young dogs who like to play
And old dogs who like to lay.

There's normal dogs who play and sleep
And strange dogs who walk on two feet.

There's dogs who like to sleep
And dogs who like to peep.

There's fat dogs who like to wink
And thin dogs who like to sprint.

Kirsty Galliers (11)
Colburn CP School

PURPLE

Purple is friendly advice,
Purple is a loving cuddle,
Purple is a cosy blanket,
Purple is a nice surprise.

Purple is a bad excuse,
Purple is an angry planet,
Purple is a horrible mess,
Purple is a very bad guess.

Calin Bousfield (10)
Colburn CP School

THE SUN

The sun is the king of all he surveys,
The Emperor of the sky,
God of all gods,
The Zeus, the Osiris, the Thor of his time
And then he looks up to the God of the night.

Martin Rooney (11)
Colburn CP School

AUTUMN

A   curling branch bangs to the ground
U   nder trees shiny conkers fall
T   he howling wind snaps acorns
U   nderneath the clouds a rushing mist blows
M   y feet walk on leaves with a crunch
N   asty weather starts.

Holly Magoolagan (9)
Cracoe & Rylstone Primary School

MY PUPPY BAILEY

He's very playful, never stops,
He eats so much he might go pop.
Chewing everything in his sight,
Sometimes he howls all through the night.
Cheeky, noisy, and always sniffing,
An early riser, doesn't know what he's missing!
A fast runner and he jumps up,
He's a cute, fluffy, golden pup!
A waggy tail and huge paws,
He scratches hard at the back door.
In the garden he runs off,
Sometimes I worry he might get lost!
When we've got tea and he wants some too,
We put down his food and that will have to do.
And when he gets sleepy at the end of the day,
We put him to bed and hope there he will stay!

Jessica Healy (11)
Cracoe & Rylstone Primary School

AUTUMN

Crunching	One
Rustling	Two
Autumn	Three
Leaves	Watch
Roll	All
Along	The
Slowly	Leaves
With the	Blow
Autumn	Right
Breeze	Past
Gentle wind	Me.

Richard Armstrong (10)
Cracoe & Rylstone Primary School

ALL THE ANIMALS

'Moo!' said the silly cow,
'Oink!' said the pig.
'Quack!' said the little duck,
                running in its pen.

'Buzz!' said the bumblebee,
'Croak!' said the frog.
'Woof!' said the naughty dog,
                sleeping in its bed.

'Miaow!' the cat cried.
The bird began to chirp
and all at once the sheep began to
'Baa!' so that they could all be heard.

Amie Hargreaves (11)
Cracoe & Rylstone Primary School

THE SEA

Seaweed sways and swerves
fish swim and play
they go round in curves
people lie in the bay
see a glint of fish
sunlight sparkles on their skin
people eat them on a dish.

Laurie Keegan & Emily Wilson (9)
Cracoe & Rylstone Primary School

2000 YEARS

Over the past 2000 years,
A lot has happened, took place, occurred,
Henry VIII, Victorians, monks,
Seventies' swingers, rock stars, punks,
Nelson Mandela, men on the moon,
Aliens may be coming soon?
The Black Death and World War One,
Computers and the CD rom,
Education, women's rights,
Sailing ships and Bonfire Nights,
Vikings, Normans, all of them,
Since Christ was born in Bethlehem.

Rebecca Carlisle (11)
Cracoe & Rylstone Primary School

A POEM ABOUT AUTUMN

The wind loops, howls, roars,
Hedgehogs hibernate and the fruit gets harvested,
Trees squeak when breezes blow,
Leaves, amber, ruby, gold,
Tiptoe quietly and crackle crisp, cold,
Acorns, conkers on the ground roll around,
Dewdrops sparkle in the morning sun,
The frost bites sharply.

Amanda Steele (11)
Cracoe & Rylstone Primary School

CATS

Cats sleep
Cats snore
Cats scratch
With their claws.

Cats squeak
Cats peep
Cats sneak in
Between your feet.

Megan Darbyshire (10)
Cracoe & Rylstone Primary School

SNOWDROP

Here I am.
Deep in the ground.
Been in the ground waiting for a sign of spring.
I've been pushing, pushing all the time.
Here I am popping up, hunting for life and light.
I'm lonely no friends around me.
But they will pop up one day.
Oh that journey it was tough.
But now I'm in the light with no friends.
I had a surprise, more snowdrops were growing.
I wasn't lonely any more
I was playing with other snowdrops.
Some days we fight winds.

Henry Anderson (8)
Hackforth & Hornby CE School

SNOWDROPS

I am a tiny little bulb.
Now I am coming through like a shot.
Now I am telling you that spring is coming.
I am out and I am ready for it.
I have been waiting to get out of that dark, dingy floor.
It is great to see the light again.
I have a beautiful middle for the bees' honey.

Michael Metcalfe (9)
Hackforth & Hornby CE School

SNOWDROP

The snowdrop is pretty.
The snowdrop is sitting under the ground
and it is dark.

I am the first snowdrop to pop up.
I am all white and I have a bit of green.

The snowdrop is soft.

Samantha Stirk (7)
Hackforth & Hornby CE School

SNOWDROP

Deep down in the frightening dungeons of the ground,
There was a cute little bulb that was crippled up.
Struggling to earth and suddenly it popped up!
Then it made way for its pretty petals that were white and green.
Suddenly it opened its snowball head.

Matthew Donaldson (7)
Hackforth & Hornby CE School

SNOWDROP

There is a snowdrop down deep in the ground.
Waiting and waiting.
The messenger.
Then suddenly it feels the sun's warmth.
It decided to pop up from out of the ground.
It pushed and pushed, up and up.
Out of the ground out to the sun.
That night it was windy and the wind blew round and round.
The little snowdrop fought and fought and tried to keep up
                                          against the wind.
He did it all night and never stopped.
That night was a horrible night.
But he stayed, *yes* he stayed.

Mary Rose Ropner (8)
Hackforth & Hornby CE School

SNOWDROPS

I was waiting for spring and was bored.

Suddenly I started to struggle and struggle.
All the rocks fell down on me
And in a twinkle I was up.

I was so pleased that I was not bored anymore
And everyone was looking at me.
It was a bit strange.

I like it now, it is not strange
And all the other ones like it.

Sam Williamson (7)
Hackforth & Hornby CE School

SNOWDROP

Snowdrop sitting underground.
Waiting, waiting for the sign of spring.
So lonely down there.
Finally he picks a time
To sprout with his group,
Not daring to go alone.
Once he's up he's blown around
But too strong to fall.
Swaying around and around.
Then the wind stops and apologises.
And the wind says he will allow the spring to come.
Finally the spring comes.
Time for me to go.
Bye, bye.

Letitia Thomas (1)
Hackforth & Hornby CE School

SNOWDROPS

I am bored in a dark, dark ground.

One day I knew it was time to come out.

So I pushed and slammed and then I was out.

When I was out I was having a good time.

Everyone knew that I was a sign of spring.

Spring arrived and they knew I was I sign of spring.

Thomas Lockhart (8)
Hackforth & Hornby CE School

SNOWDROP

Waiting, waiting and waiting.
In the dark, black ground.
Then suddenly I shouted it must be spring.
I turned and twisted, missing stones
And shot up from the ground.
My friends were there it was worth it.
My petals started to grow.
My stem got longer and longer.
The spring was long
And I started to die but I will be there.
Next spring.

Oliver Milverton (9)
Hackforth & Hornby CE School

SNOWDROP

Here I come,
Popping up.
Out of the dark, grey ground.
Here I come,
Shooting up.
Up to the sunlight above.
I'm coming out.
I'm out again
To the Earth above.
I'm enjoying myself,
I'm enjoying myself very much,
With all my heart I'm loving it.

Alice Milverton (8)
Hackforth & Hornby CE School

SNOWDROPS

Here I am.
Stuck under the mud.
Trying to push up from the mud.
Push, push, hello everybody.
I have pretty white sweet petals.
I have small white petals with green smiley faces.
I have a lovely yellow and orange sweetcorn.
All my friends and family are here.
All my family are the same as me
I am soft and strong and fragile.

Charlotte Hurworth (9)
Hackforth & Hornby CE School

SNOWDROPS

Here I am
Stuck in the dark, deep, cold earth
Trying to pop up to tell you that spring is on its way.
Now I am starting my horrendous journey.
I pop up through a gap it is great to see light.
Now I have lovely white petals and a bright yellow middle.

Tanya Stirk (9)
Hackforth & Hornby CE School

FLOWER

I'm underground
I am waiting.
Without a crown
I am sprouting.

Here I come
Like a baby
I've got no mum
A sad baby.

I haven't got a pretty flower
I am waiting
I shall have one in an hour
Now I've got one.

I'm a snowdrop
I am pretty
I am fragile
But I am strong.

I am dying
Now it's summer
Next year I'll come
As good as new.

Edward Blows (8)
Hackforth & Hornby CE School

DOGGY BUSINESS

My dog Benji cries at my door!
Early in the morning waiting for attention
He follows me down for breakfast to eat his with me
When I'm at home he starts to spring about
But when he's alone he starts to cry.

Kieran Garnett (9)
Hambleton CE Primary School

SEASONS

Spring is beginning to go wild,
The sun drifting lazily up to burning point.
Flowers blooming all around,
Mothers dead-heading daffodils dreamily,
Nights gradually diminishing.

Summer erupting with heat and pleasure,
The sun scorching your skin unbearably,
Desperately trying to keep plants and flowers alive,
Drinking pints and pints of water,
Sitting on deckchairs relaxing.

Autumn the trees are ladened with fruit and nuts,
Fields filled with swaying corn,
Birds swooping noiselessly away,
A multicoloured carpet of leaves covers the ground.

Winter turning everyone's spirits down,
Making days shrink unhurriedly,
Settling snow on every surface possible
Turning the sky a murky grey.

Harriet Andrews (8)
Hambleton CE Primary School

SWEETS

The world would be a better place,
If we could have more sweets.
More chocolate eggs and candy sticks,
More sherbet dips to lick.
That would be my perfect world,
If we could have more treats.

Helen Bond (8)
Hambleton CE Primary School

DALMATIAN

Blotches on the elegant Dalmatian,
As the beautiful dog strolls
His gigantic brown eyes look at me,
That's my friend.

He bounds along and jumps at me,
As I throw a ball to play,
His tail is always wagging,
That's my friend.

We walk along the paths together,
His head is held high,
He is so springy when he moves
That's my friend.

We are in the house together,
So cosy and so warm,
I'm glad I've got my dog
That's my friend.

Kimberley Pattison (9)
Hambleton CE Primary School

OWLS

A shadow circles the ground,
As the owl swoops down
A mouse sprints for cover.
But it's too late!
As the owl snatches its prey
It swiftly glides to a tree with the mouse
Surveying for danger before soaring back to its territory.

Josh Cripps (9)
Hambleton CE Primary School

MY DOGS

I have three fluffy dogs
Called Zara, Ben and Jack.
Some of my friends would like to take them
                           home with them.
Jack and Ben guard the house.
But are frightened if they see a mouse!
Zara does not care for mice,
She thinks they're not very nice.

Cats have to run,
Zara thinks that's good fun.
They all love to play hide and seek
Around the garden and up the creek.
Jack barks at cats, rats and bats!
Whilst Zara and Ben bark at people in hats!
They all love to play with me,
But eventually I have to go home for tea.

Elizabeth Richardson (8)
Hambleton CE Primary School

SPRINGTIME

It's time for the Easter Bunny,
It's time for bees to make honey.
The flowers will start to bloom,
We will be rid of the winter gloom.
Birds will make their nests,
The trees have had their rests.
The sun will send down a yellow ray,
And we will shout hip, hip hooray.

The days will be light,
No more dark night.
More time for fun,
Under the spring sun.
People will be pleased,
Now the winter has ceased.
Blue skies to be seen,
And gardens full of green.

That's springtime.

Steven Nix (9)
Hambleton CE Primary School

SUPER KEV TO THE RESCUE

Through midfield
And past all the team,
There goes Super Kev
As if it were a dram.

He takes a shot
From the halfway line,
It's lined up for a goal
And it goes in fine.

The sound of the whistle
Silences the crowd
They look in amazement
As the goal is disallowed.

Then everyone boos
And shouts at the ref,
It was disallowed
Because of the goalie's death.

Lee Emmerson (10)
Hambleton CE Primary School

THUNDERSTORM

Pearls of raindrops shimmer on the windowpane.
They trickle down the transparent glass delicately.
Then the sky suddenly lights up,
With the dazzle of the lightning.

It fills the sky with wonder and light.
Then, thunder roars and makes the sky tremble with fear.
People hibernate under their snugly covers
Thinking they'll be safe.

The next roar of thunder blazes the sky in half.
Raindrops still tap on the window in a beat.
The next clash of thunder,
Illuminates the sky.

Will it ever stop?

Emily Palmer (9)
Hambleton CE Primary School

THE LION

Great big fangs,
Long sharp claws,
A swishy tail,
And four huge paws.

A long tangly mane,
Green glaring eyes,
He's the king of the jungle,
You should see his size.

Alice Leake (8)
Hambleton CE Primary School

THE OWL

As darkness falls,
The harsh screech of the snowy owl
Is heard through the isolated forest.
His piercing eyes,
Watching the golden carpet of the forest floor
For any unsuspecting creatures.
The ghostly white form silently swoops,
Grasping his prey in sharp dagger-like talons.
Coming to rest in the secluded spot,
Where the glistening moonlight dances with the trees.
He rips and tears at the flesh,
Until his meal is over.
He returns to his hunting.
His piercing eyes disappear in the darkness of the night.

Hayley Bell (9)
Hambleton CE Primary School

MIDNIGHT THUNDER

The droplets blend elegantly down the windowpane,
Thunder booms out in the pearly sky.
Hiding under the warm, comfy covers,
The patting echoes of dripping rain fall outside.

The dynamic flashing illuminates the night sky,
A movement of the shadowed trees catches my eye.
The dynamic crashing fearfully gets harder,
The pattering rain gets accompanied, a hand touches the side of me.

A cool shiver runs down my spine.

Shelley Hobson (9)
Hambleton CE Primary School

SPORTS

I like,
Rugby fast and rough,
Football quick and tough,
Swimming speedy and hard
Unlike the steady games of cards.

I think,
A game of tennis is cool,
Motor racing and the smell of fuel,
Basketball I like the best,
Because it's better than all the rest.

Daniel Kneen (8)
Hambleton CE Primary School

THUNDER AND LIGHTNING

I curl up in my heated bed
As the light glistens in my room
Each corner becomes a million stars
As the lightning starts to take over
I can hear the falling of the droplets
Tapping softly on my window
Then comes the roaring of the thunder
Banging on the glass
I shiver with fright
As the roaring night gently fades away
I pull my covers up over my head
And hibernate
Waiting for the monsters to leave.

Luke Ryans (10)
Hambleton CE Primary School

THUNDERSTORM

Droplets
Water droplets drumming on the glass
Water beads make a maze on the pane,
Slowly dissolving from the puddles,
The sky become quiet again.

Thunder
The orchestral sound of drums being played,
Hard and furiously,
As the thunder crashes,
An enormous sound.

Lightning
The vicious jagged streaks highlight the windows,
The glittering flashes brighten the sky,
As the thunder starts to fade away,
The town becomes silent . . .

Kirsty Mycoe (8)
Hambleton CE Primary School

MY HERO

James Bond is my greatest hero of them all,
He's very dark and very tall,
When someone tries to mess him about
He takes out his gun and blacks them all out.

So as he's mighty and very strong,
He has a movie with a great song,
He's also on worldwide TV,
And definitely the hero for me.

Jane Bond (8)
Hambleton CE Primary School

WHAT IS IT?

Round and chubby
Toothless and gummy
Noisy and gurgly.

Can you guess?

Pretty and sweet,
Tiny little feet.
Sometimes awake,
Sometimes asleep.
Splashing in the bath.
Crawling on the mat.
It's a lovely smiling

Baby!

Abigail Jones (10)
Hambleton CE Primary School

LOOK UP

If you look up in the sky,
you'll see a spaceship and wonder why.
A rocket zooms up round,
at the end of the day it lands safely on the ground.
Out comes James, Frankie, Sammy and Bob,
they're tired and weary but they've not finished the job.
In the morning they shall rise,
up into those misty skies.
In the morning they shall face,
the ghastly fate of outer space.

Lucy Whitehead (9)
Hambleton CE Primary School

A SPACEMAN

I'd like to be a spaceman
I'd like to ride up high
To visit other planets
And stars that catch my eye.

The world would seem so different
Once I'd been in space
And seen the world in miniature
No bigger than my face

If only it was possible
It would be so much fun
To leave the Earth and come back again
Come back to see my mum!

Luke Roberts (9)
Hambleton CE Primary School

MY BROTHER AND I

I have a brother who's twelve you see,
He's only three years older than me.
We're quite the same in a lot of ways
Well, that's what everyone else says.
I have brown eyes, he has blue,
He likes to fish and I do too.
We don't always agree when playing our games,
Sometimes calling each other names.
But even though we argue and fight
As brothers go, he's alright!

Gareth Thirlwell (9)
Hambleton CE Primary School

MY BIG SISTER

My big sister was having a party
There was a knock at the door at twenty to four.

I was just about to open it when . . .
She whispered, 'Go away!'

The girls began to arrive with presents and cards,
There were big ones, small ones, long ones,
Thin ones all with bows.

I was just about to say
Is there one for me when . . .
She said, 'Go away!'

There was dancing, singing and laughing,
While Mum was sticking sausages on sticks.
I was just about to dance when . . .
She shouted, *'Go away!'*

They all gathered round the table
Where there was food for all;
Paper plates; hands everywhere
Sausage rolls, crisps and sweets.

I was just about to grab my plate when . . .
She yelled, *'Go away!'*

'Time for the candles,' shouted Mum.
'Girls, girls, gather round, let's sing.'
I was just about to say, when . . .

She said, 'Come little sis stand with me.'

Gemma Greener (10)
Hambleton CE Primary School

THE THUNDERSTORM

The transparent droplets, drumming on tiny windows,
Sparks of lightning across the midnight sky.
The piercing sound of the thunder outside,
Bursts of sweat from my eyebrows trickle down my cheeks,
Wondering what will happen next.

Suddenly the sky illuminates with lightning.
As the sky calms down the terrifying roar of the thunder
                                        claps once more.
The sky is still once again.

Alice Gibbs (8)
Hambleton CE Primary School

THE TALKING JELLY

I went to my friends and she said,
'I have a picnic for us.'
She put it in the garden
Then the basket said, 'Pardon.'
The sandwich started talking to the jelly.
It said 'Shaking jelly
In my belly makes you go all smelly.'
I had a bit of jelly it started speaking to my tummy
And it said 'Yummy, yummy.'

Hope Boscock (7)
Horton in Ribblesdale CE Primary School

MY RABBIT'S AWFUL HABITS

My rabbit has an awful habit.
It chews up plastic bags.

And then in summer
It got even dumber.
It pulled the bed covers off the beds.

The next day
There it lay
On my bedroom floor
And then it was sick
On the bathroom door.

Then I took him to the vets
There I saw tons of pets.
And that was when Sutty escaped
Right outside the garden gates.

I ran and ran
Just like a van.
Will I find him?
I hope I can.

Karen Lambert (7)
Horton in Ribblesdale CE Primary School

WIZZ THE SPACESHIP

Zooming here and zooming there.
Wizz the spaceship is zooming everywhere.
Zooms over here.
He zooms over there.
Wizz zooms everywhere.

Another spaceship came and said,
'You need to slow down.'
Wizz the spaceship ignored him
And bang he crashed.

Ethan Boocock (9)
Horton in Ribblesdale CE Primary School

MR ONE EYE'S STRANGE EXPERIENCE

One day captain Greenbeard saw
Jimmy standing outside the door.
'What's up Captain?' Greenbeard said.
Jimmy frowned and hung his head.
'It's Mr One Eye,' Jimmy sighed.
'I'm afraid he's lost his other eye!'
And so he had
How very sad
Then Mr Tubbs came walking by
It seemed like he had stolen the eye.

Then the next day
They sailed away
To the land of Bongily Boo
There they found
Without a sound
A dirty old sack
Inside they saw One Eye's eye.
So they gave him it back
Now he could see
He found his pet bee!

Beth Algie (10)
Horton in Ribblesdale CE Primary School

BEANIES

B eanies, Beanies they can beat
E very one in the street
A nyway they are the best
   they can always beat the rest
N ever will they make a mess
   or else they will get paid less
I would never hate a beanie
   cos I am very keen
E very time I give them a cuddle
   they will always get in a muddle
S till when they go on holiday they will send
   me a letter (only pretend)

   The end.

Holly Connaughton (9)
Horton in Ribblesdale CE Primary School

BUNS ARE FUN

My mum is such fun
She gives me a bun
Just before my dinner.
The buns are so yummy
They're good for your tummy
And that's what happens at dinner time.

Matthew Holgate (9)
Horton in Ribblesdale CE Primary School

GHOSTS 'N' GHOULS

Ghosts 'n' ghouls
are only for fools.
They're just a load of rubbish.

Vampires dripping deep red blood
from their pale white, jagged fangs.

Don't be afraid of the Boogie Man
or in the night those *big, loud bangs!*

I'm not afraid and I never will be.
Never
    ever
        ever.

Katie Fox (10)
Horton in Ribblesdale CE Primary School

OWLS IN THE NIGHT

The sun is asleep
The moon is awake
The owl swoops over the glittering lake.
In the moon his eyes shine bright
He gives the mice a terrible fright.

The owl is swooping
It catches a mouse.
Then flies through the darkness
Back to his house.

Jessie Alston (10)
Horton in Ribblesdale CE Primary School

ALIENS IN OUR SCHOOL

Clanging, banging, tanning, what's coming?
Bang, clang!
Out he comes hear him clang and bang.
There my . . . my *bang!*
I doubt this is about the millennium.
Wish, swoosh, wash this, wash that.
Go out and about
The children came close
Suddenly . . .
Bye, bye.
With a gush and a whoosh they were gone.
What was that, what was what?

Becky Wilcock (8)
Horton in Ribblesdale CE Primary School

RONNY THE RAT

Oh Ronny the rat shut up!
Oh Ronny the rat go away!
Oh Ronny the rat stop eating that mat!
Oh Ronny the rat you are very very fat from that mat.
Oh Ronny the rat you're such a little prat!
Oh Ronny the rat stop tormenting that cat!
Oh Ronny the rat stop eating that cheese and *Bang!*
He was a white as a ghost.

Steven Millman (8)
Horton in Ribblesdale CE Primary School

KILNSEY SHOW - MILLENNIUM DOME

Kilnsey show,
muddy, fun,
bouncing, jumping, judging,
tents, games - body zone, queues,
deafening, bragging, boasting,
costly, crowded,
Millennium Dome.

Bianca Briggs (7)
Kettlewell School

UNTITLED

Village
peaceful, alone,
waiting, huddling, caring,
corner shops - streets, superstores
smelling, deafening, crowding,
crazy, loud
City

Edward Hird (9)
Kettlewell School

UNTITLED

Kettlewell;
peaceful, beautiful,
sharing, caring, sheltering,
walks, hills - shops, skyscrapers,
deafening, polluting, pushing,
busy, massive;
London.

Hannah Locker (7)
Kettlewell School

HAMLETS AND CITIES

Hamlet,
small, quiet,
nestling, hiding, sleeping
streams, cottages - cars, lorries
deafening, polluting, stinking
noisy, busy,
City

Iona Wood-Katic (10)
Kettlewell School

KETTLEWELL - LONDON

Kettlewell,
peaceful, magical
exciting, caring, welcoming
fields, trees - roads, cars
bustling, bulging, deafening
lively, loud,
London

Tiffany Briggs (10)
Kettlewell School

DALES RAMBLERS

Ramblers
fit, daring
walking, climbing, viewing
rucksacks, boots - cars, trucks
beeping, speeding, screeching
noisy, lazy
Drivers.

Andrew Mallinson (9)
Kettlewell School

COUNTRY TO TOWN

Dales village,
quiet, peaceful,
thriving, exciting, welcoming
pubs, space - skyscrapers, workers
polluting, hooting, rushing,
busy, loud,
City.

Iain Howarth (9)
Kettlewell School

UNTITLED

Gamekeeper,
active, athletic,
watching, listening, protecting
dogs, birds - traps, guns
pouncing, creeping, scheming,
sneaky, devious,
Poacher.

Amie Locker (10)
Kettlewell School

UNTITLED

Gamekeeper,
alert, sharp
watching, waiting, whiling away his time,
ferrets, dogs - guns, snares,
lurking, killing, creeping
sneaky, camouflaged,
Poacher.

Emily Rackham (9)
Kettlewell School

MY BIRDY TREE

My Birdy Tree,
Rough,
Prickly,
Spooky,
Very high
And freezing.
Blowing
Branches,
Leaves to
Keep me warm.
Bugs to eat,
Rain on the
Green grass.
Friends over
To say hello

Philippa Mallinson (6)
Kettlewell School

GOOD OLD KETTLEWELL

Kettlewell,
hilly, picturesque,
sheltering, thriving, enchanting
scarecrows, inns - superstores, traffic
roaring, buzzing, deafening,
dangerous, loud,
London.

Simon Johnston (9)
Kettlewell School

MY HEDGEHOG

My Hedgehog
Sees
Gloomy skies,
Spooky people,
Very damp
Soft earth.
Lots of snow,
Rocky walls,
Low ground.
My dale.

Harriet Rackham (6)
Kettlewell School

MY HOME

My home
Blue is everywhere,
Leaves floating,
Sand lays wet,
Rocks falling,
Flowers growing.
A Dale's pond.

James Middleton (7)
Kettlewell School

A RABBIT'S DALE

A rabbit's Dale
Giant people,
Nasty rain,
Shiny river,
Children
Playing.
Cows,
Sheep,
Donkeys,
My friends.
Hard rocks,
Green grass,
Brown and
Green trees.

David Hird (5)
Kettlewell School

A DALE'S RABBIT

A Dale's rabbit
I see,
Cars driving,
White sheep eating grass,
Nettles beside me
Petals touching the wall,
Fields with cows in.

Harvey Briggs (4)
Kettlewell School

WHAT IS BLUE?

What is blue?
The sea is blue
Splashing along the seashore.

What is gold?
Jewels are gold
Sparkling and twinkling.

What is silver?
Paperclips are silver
Shining on my piece of paper.

What is green?
The grass is green
Tickling the sunflowers.

What is ginger?
A cat is ginger
Purring on the stairs.

Sarah Hill (7)
Knayton CE Primary School

MY ACCIDENTS

When it was time to get out of bed
I came downstairs and banged my head.

I went upstairs and I looked back
Then I got my finger stuck in the tap.

I ran downstairs into the hall
Then I fell over a ball.

I went to play with my bunny
It bit my finger, and it wasn't funny.

Robin Cook (7)
Knayton CE Primary School

WHAT IS RED?

What is red?
A red sunset
Glowing in the sky.

What is gold?
A goldfish
Swimming in the water.

What is brown?
A brown horse
Walking to the field.

What is blue?
A blue car
On the road.

What is yellow?
The sun is yellow
In the sky.

What is white?
The clouds are white
Floating in the sky.

Sam Looker (8)
Knayton CE Primary School

THE TREE

There was once a wonderful tree,
That fell down, it was two hundred and three.
My mum was mad,
My dad was glad,
But my sister was cross with me.

Matthew Wingrove (9)
Knayton CE Primary School

THE OLD OAK TREE

There was once a beautiful big oak tree.
It stood at the top of the hill.
When I go to school I'm always late,
Because I go and see it every day.
Sometimes I scramble up it
And feel the lovely, wrinkly leaves,
All crisp and wavy.
Sometimes in different places it feels quite spiky.

I love to see it just standing there.
I say in my mind 'Are you lonely?'
I always go and talk to it every day.
I never forget the tree even when I go on
Holiday.
It's a wonderful tree everyone says so,
And I made a treehouse out of it.

I love that oak tree!

Jessica Jenyns (9)
Knayton CE Primary School

THE MAGIC TREE

One day I found a big tree.
It started to talk
And it made me jump.
It said, 'Have a wish'
In a very loud voice.
'I wish to be a princess in an immense castle', I said.
I never got my wish.
And I never saw the tree again.

Stephanie Christon (9)
Knayton CE Primary School

A Jungle Palm Tree

A microscopic tree was sitting in the corner of a jungle.
I went close, it had a mumble.
I climbed up, it had a tiger inside.
I had a look, it was pin-sized.
I went to another palm tree, it squawked.
I went up again, it talked.
Owls howled in the night.
I will scream, I might.
I went to smell both of the trees.
I saw a honeycomb there for bees.
I got a fishing rod.
I named my toad Tod.

Olivia Bentley (8)
Knayton CE Primary School

What Is Yellow?

What is yellow?
The sun is yellow
Shining in the sky.

What is blue?
The sky is blue
With sparkly stars in it.

What is brown?
My pony is brown
Streaming her tail in the wind.

Sarah Coidan (6)
Knayton CE Primary School

THE WINDING WILLOW

My tree is gnarled,
It hides near a hut.
My dad thinks it's old,
And needs cutting up.
But I say 'No Dad don't cut it down,'
I climb and play until the end of day.

I went up to bed,
Early one night,
And heard a sound,
I jumped with fright.
But out of my window there was no tree,
And it scared the life out of me.

I miss my old tree,
The way that it stands,
Gone forever,
No longer it's grand.
I sit all day crying,
By the hut on my swing,
I love my poor tree, give it back to me.

Rosalyn Mogridge (8)
Knayton CE Primary School

MY IMAGINARY TREE . . .

The tree I imagine is a marvellous tree,
It hides great surprises and dreams for me.
When I'm asleep all snuggled up
In my bed,
My vast tree brings dreams
To my tired head.
The sweets are amazing
To good to be true,
But something horrid happened
Between me and you.
One night as I climbed our
Huge, steep steps,
The magical dream that I had
So very long kept.
Disappeared so quickly
From my weary head,
My beige looming tree
Was now truly dead.
That night I woke up
And outside my window,
Was my immense tree, with
Its beautiful gleaming glow.
The tree I imagine is a marvellous tree,
It hides great surprises and dreams for me.

Laura Keast (9)
Knayton CE Primary School

There Was Once A Tree

There was once a tree,
Which was gnarled and stiff,
Which had a ring of toadstools around it.

There was once a tree
Which was huge and looming,
The branches looked like arms which were going to make me
Burst into laughter.

There was once a tree which was tearful and sad,
It is now brown and wrinkled.

There was once a tree which was happy in spring.

Lorna Spence (8)
Knayton CE Primary School

The Tree

Trees are fun you can make dens in them.
Trees squiggle and wiggle in the wind when it
blows.
The branches are like swiping wings,
Like swords in a battle.
The branches sway up and down,
Flowing like a river.
A trickle of sap runs down the tree
And sets solidly.

Tom Harrison (9)
Knayton CE Primary School

THE TREE DEN IN THE GLEN

There was once a boy,
Who played with his toys.
A man came along and said,
'Can we have that tree?'
The boy said, 'No, it's precious to me.'
'You cannot take it for the den in the glen,
The tree is for play, so never!'
The tree rattles in the night,
It gives me a fright.
'Don't take my tree.'
The den is dark and gloomy,
With a box that's quite loomy.
'Don't take my tree!'
The garden will look bare,
With nothing to wear.
'Don't take my tree!'

Oliver Morgan-Williams (9)
Knayton CE Primary School

THE SECRET TREE DEN

In the den there are arched trees and branches
The trees above your head are 50 feet tall,
But if you don't want to go right, you can go left,
If you go left you will see long, dangling ivy which is strong.
In summer the den is full of joy and it is camouflaged.
In winter the den is flooded with snow.
In the morning I get dressed as quickly as I can,
Because I want to get to my den.
If I am upset or angry I run to my den.

Gavin Lovell (8)
Knayton CE Primary School

THE TREE

There was once a really gnarled tree.
It always stood in the centre of the garden.
This tree was a hundred years old.
It seemed sharp so it's told.
It was blind because it did not know how to dance,
It had no mind.
The tree had to stay in its roots because it had no push-up
boots.
The poor old tree had no friends because it kept blocking
all the bends.
The poor beige-red tree found a wife, but she had to make
a sacrifice,
For her best tree in all the world.

John Tough (9)
Knayton CE Primary School

MY TREE

It is furry and silky
It looks grey and silvery
And it shimmers in the sun.

It's pale and small it's
Narrow and looming
And it dances in the breeze.

It's sweet and tender
It's really quite nice
I like the colour and
Touch with the wrinkly leaves.

Laura Roberts (8)
Knayton CE Primary School

THE SPARKLY PALM TREE

I was in bed one night,
When I thought
What is that?
I looked out of my window and there was a tree,
I said 'Well, that tree was not there a minute ago.'
It was a lovely scary palm tree.
I went downstairs and said
'Mum can you get palm trees in this country?'
'No, go to bed',
So, I went to bed.
I tried to get to sleep.
Well could it be my dream
Or is it real?
I crept down
Out of the door,
And there stood a sparkly palm tree.
The coconuts were glittering and inside were chocolates
And sweets.

Kate Ward (9)
Knayton CE Primary School

THE TREE

There is a tree
And it is enormous
The leaves are green
The trunk is terracotta.

The tree is really tall
We all climb on the tree
And play all day
We make a den in the tree.

We play in the den
All sorts of games
All sorts of things
We really like our den.

Our tree is very old
It has lots of wrinkles
Looming branches all above
Us like spooky hands.

Charlotte Muxlow (8)
Knayton CE Primary School

RICE KRISPIES AND FISH

The thing I like best in my house is my fish.
Not my mum
Not my dad
Just my fish.
No pain, no worries,
Always under my control.
Snap, Crackle and Pop are their names.
Though they never eat any.
Snap is thin, Crackle is fat,
Pop is even fatter.
Snap likes fun, Crackle likes to stay in one place,
But Pop likes to be in his own space.

Sophie Meredith (9)
Langcliffe County Primary School

OUT IN THE SUN

Out in the sun,
Sat on a bench
Under the old oak tree,
Reading a book,
Drinking a cup of tea.

Out in the sun,
Sat on a bench
Under the old oak tree,
Barking I hear
From kennels near,
Now I'm drinking my cup of tea.

Out in the sun,
Sat on a bench
Under the old oak tree,
Next to my dog
That's jumped in a bog,
And knocked over my cup of tea.

Andrew Jeffrey (10)
Langcliffe County Primary School

MILLENNIUM MARK

I know a man called Millennium Mark,
When he's bored he sits in the park.
One mysterious day he went the wrong way
And found himself smothered in bundles of hay.

I know a man called Millennium Mark,
He works in a shop as an office clerk.
He went to work one day and collected little pay
And asked the governor if he had anything to say.

I know a man called Millennium Mark,
He always goes to the animal ark.
He takes his friend Jay, whose best friend is May
And after they go swimming down by the bay.

I know a man called Millennium Mark,
Who is afraid of the dreadful dark.
He curled in a corner with nothing to say
And that's where the old man decided to stay.

Nadine Milligan & Oriana Smith (11)
Le Cateau Primary School

I Saw a . . .

I saw a tiger go to the shop,
I saw a cheetah doing the hop,
I saw an elephant go pop,
I saw a gorilla dressed as a cop,
I saw a dog talking to a frog,
I saw a hippo balanced on a log,
I saw a peacock going for a jog,
I saw a rabbit eating like a hog,
I saw a goldfish eating a bit of cod,
I saw a pig praying to God,
I saw a giraffe having a nod,
I saw a Martian landing a pod,
I saw an alligator on a hike,
I saw a whale dancing with a pike,
I saw a mouse on a bike,
I saw a chipmunk acting like a tyke,
I saw a cow jump over the moon,
I saw an owl eating his lunch at noon,
I saw a dinosaur acting like a goon,
I saw a bull singing out of tune.

George Curtis (10)
Le Cateau Primary School

Ode To An Empty Crisp Packet

Hail, O' empty crisp packet,
The way you crinkle in my ears,
It makes me feel oh so cosy.
Your shiny foil makes my bones tingle,
You make me shiver when I am in your
Elegant company.
Your tasty, cheese and onion smell
Makes me always want to be in your presence.

Never again will I crunch another crisp,
Never again will I listen to the radio
For your sound is far more astounding.
I shall always need your merry laugh
Tingling in my ears,
I will always honour you O' fine, crunchy,
Crisp packet.
Without your warm, joyful feeling,
My life would be tearful and incomplete.

Emily Marshall (10)
Le Cateau Primary School

ODE TO A HAIRBRUSH

O' hairbrush
Most beautiful thing of all
I love the way you comb my hair
Stroke by stroke
Your bristles so fine
Tackling the knots, like you were tackling the world.
You look like a million dollars
You are the most amazing thing I will ever see
You bring me so much pleasure
You are the apple of my eye
I shall never look at another hairbrush again
I'll worship you always and forever
I am dreading the day when I have to give you up
You send a shiver down my spine
You are my first love
You are my only love
I adore you more than anything else
I will never look at another comb or hairbrush again
Whenever I look at you it sends a shiver down my spine
O' hairbrush I adore you.

Michelle Allen (10)
Le Cateau Primary School

ODE TO A COMPUTER

O' computer sitting on my desk
Shiny and white and having a rest
Shall I push your button and switch you on
And listen to your beautiful whirly song?

O' computer sitting on my desk
Your games are so hard
Sometimes my brain needs a rest
Every level is new for me and you
But every day we always managed to get through
The pleasure you bring me
Fills me with delight
O' computer I dream of you at night.

O' computer sitting on my desk
We can even connect to the Internet
Travelling all around the world
Talking to lots of boys and girls.

O' computer you have a lot to give
You're amazing, terrific, such a whizz.

Scott McGuffie (10)
Le Cateau Primary School

ODE TO A BLACKBOARD

O' hail mighty blackboard
How I long to write on you.
How I long to hear the sound of you
When the chalk is scratching.
I love the smell of the remains of chalk
Lying still.
How smooth you make yourself
When I write on you.
Your beauty makes me want to worship you.

I shall never again touch another whiteboard,
I shall never again touch another slate,
I shall never again touch another piece of paper
Or pen.

Kimberley Gray (10)
Le Cateau Primary School

ODE TO A COCKROACH!

Hail, O' merry cockroach!
Most beautiful of all.
You make me want to get on my knees
And beg to you,
You smell like a freshly picked bunch of roses,
You have a smell stronger than an ant,
You sound so very gentle,
You sound just like my gran.

Never shall I buy another insect,
Never shall I swap you for any money,
Never shall I take you back to the wild,
Never shall I feed you to your enemies
And never, never shall I leave you out to die.

Please, the apple of my eye,
Stop lurking around the rubbish
And spend more time with me.

Oriana Smith (11)
Le Cateau Primary School

PLAYTIME!

Hip, hip hooray the best time of the day
when we can all go out to play,
not that I don't like school of course
but it's nice to have a little pause,
from all the hard work that we have to do
and lots of sitting quietly too.
We can run around and scream and shout
or just walk and talk and laze about,
I am sure the teachers like playtime too,
but not as much as me and you.
The bell has gone it's time to go
but we can play again tomorrow.

Fiona Hunt (11)
Le Cateau Primary School

ODE TO A FRIDGE

O' hail, almighty fridge
How I love to take food out of your body
Your structure is the most beautiful object in the house
Your colour is the most adoring ever
How your beautiful light shines upon my food
And sends a shiver up my spine
It sends my heart jumping because you keep my food safe.
Never shall I look at another fridge again
You're more beautiful than Miss World
You look like a million dollars.

Lloyd Parker (11)
Le Cateau Primary School

FIREWORKS, FIREWORKS

Fireworks, fireworks.
Come to life and light
Up in the pitch-black night.

Fireworks, fireworks.
Light up the night
With silver, yellow,
Red, pink, blue, green,
Orange, gold,
Bronze and white.

Josephine Keating (8)
Le Cateau Primary School

HORSE

I saw a horse going round a course,
Jumping over fences.
I saw a bird on a fence,
Singing all the day.
The horse ran round,
And shook the ground,
Then the bird flew away.
What a lovely race day.

Sarah Cohen (8)
Le Cateau Primary School

Up, Up And Away

Up, up and away
Went my balloon
On a windy day.

There it goes,
Glowing red,
Flying high
Above my head.

Never mind we can still have fun,
We can go to McDonald's and get
Another one.

Carley Evers (8)
Le Cateau Primary School

Ode To A PlayStation

Hail O' PlayStation
How I love to play games on you
Playing with you is what I look forward to
There are so many games to play
I am never bored
So keep your computers
Your GameBoys too
I'll stick to my PlayStation
Just like glue.

James Murray (10)
Le Cateau Primary School

ODE TO A CHAIR

Hail O' chair
How your colour is so bright
How your four legs stand up tall on the floor
When I feel you you're so smooth and cold
When I come into the room where you are standing
I want just to look at you all day.
Never shall I swing on another swing
Never shall I slide down a slide
For you, you're my heart's desire
You're my only love
When I swing on you, your legs fly up into the air
O' how I love you.

Kirsty Graham-Battersby (11)
Le Cateau Primary School

ODE TO A CAN OF COKE

O' can of Coke
How your bubbles make me fuzzle
And how your liquid is so divine.
You're my pride and joy
Every time I take a sip of you,
My heart melts.
I think of you day and night
If I lost you I would go bonkers.

William Gillan (11)
Le Cateau Primary School

ODE TO AN ANT!

Hail, O' ant.
I love the way you carry your food,
I love the way you smell of freshly made bread,
I love the way you wriggle your body as you walk,
I love the way you work all day.

I'll never touch my hamster,
Never shall I feed my fish,
Never shall I walk my dog,
Never shall I brush my cat,

As long as you're alive you're the apple of my eye.

Sarah Williams (11)
Le Cateau Primary School

LOOK

Look, look up there,
The sky is so fair,
The sun shines bright,
You can fly your kite,
But only while the weather stays right.

Look, look over there,
See that old grizzly bear,
He's got big hands, he's got big feet,
His hair's all messy,
He's not very neat.

Look, look in there,
It's a dog if you're unaware,
He's big and hairy,
His name is Spot,
He's the dog that's got the lot.

Lauren Smart (8)
Le Cateau Primary School

ODE TO A PLAYSTATION

O' dear PlayStation
Most wonderful of all
When you play games
You are a warm, cosy friend
My stomach would be empty without you
You're marvellous
You are my only desire
I adore you all of the time
You send a shiver down my spine
You are incredible each time
You send a tingle on my hand
When I touch your control.

Andrew Robson (10)
Le Cateau Primary School

ODE TO A FRIDGE

I love to take food from your body,
I adore the way you gently purr as I open your door,
You are my heart's desire, I long to put you in my bedroom,
The beauty of your white outside sends a shiver down my spine.
When I open your door I smell the marvellous food,
Never shall I look at or touch another fridge,
I never ever want the day to come when I have to replace you,
I'm saving a place in the garden for you to be buried in,
Without you I would go mad,
Nothing has greater beauty than you.

George Curtis (10)
Le Cateau Primary School

BLOOD BROTHERS

We're the best of friends,
We're pals for good.
We're blood brothers,
But we don't like blood.
So, as tomatoes are just as red,
We're ketchup brothers instead.

Marianne Best (10)
Le Cateau Primary School

WHAT IS . . .

What is sunshine?
What is rain?
What is real in this artificial land?
I don't know.

Artificial sunshine, artificial rain,
Artificial flowers, artificial grain,
What is hot?
What is cold?
What is natural in this unreal land?
I don't know.

Plastic surgery, plastic flowers,
Virtual reality to spend our leisure hours,
What is good?
What is bad?
What is true in this artificial land?
I don't know.

What is wild?
What is free?
Who is the prisoner, you or me?
What is natural, what is real?
What are we supposed to know or feel?
I don't know.

Jamie Gareth Lewis (9)
Roecliffe CE Primary School

AN IMAGINARY WORLD

An imaginary world in outer space.
Pink and purple it can change its shape.
The people there are blue and green.
Its the weirdest place you've ever seen.
The weather can change every day,
Wind in June, snow in May.
What about animals, do they roam free?
Go wherever they want to be.
People are kind and understand each other.
Treat a foreigner like their brother.
An imaginary world in outer space.
Nobody arguing about each different race.
People exploring wherever they fly,
Discovering new places throughout the sky,
But would we really want to leave?
A green, peaceful planet all covered in trees,
Our familiar houses, our comfortable beds,
Our friend, our family, a roof over our heads,
Reassuring and kind.
Much better than an imaginary world, locked
Inside my head.

Hollie Bramley (10)
Roecliffe CE Primary School

THE SEA

The Titanic was a brilliant boat
But it hit an iceberg and couldn't stay afloat,
The sea covers seven-tenths of our planet
It claims bodies and ships and everything on it
The sea can be calm and gentle and blue,
Or white and bright, full of icicles too.
We can play and have fun and jump over waves
But beware when it storms in a terrible rage
It can claim Uncle Tom Cobbley, young people and old
Full of whales, killer sharks, sunken treasure and gold,
Coral, fish, sunken ships, mermaids, crabs, lobsters too.
On calm, sunny days its reflection is blue
But beware of the storm when it eats me and you.

Ben Wilson (9)
Roecliffe CE Primary School

WOODLOUSE

Shelled-pest,
Rock-creeper,
Pathetic-creature,
Dirt-eater,
Annoying-intruder.

It's
    A
         Woodlouse.

Henry Whittington (10)
St Mary's RC School, Malton

PET DOGS

Dogs are my best pets,
I adore their fur,
I feel angry when my pet goes to the vet,
I am very angry when dogs die,
I would feel very worried if my dog died,
So I am *really* sad, when dogs die.

Dogs die every year,
It's really sad when your dog dies,
Every time of the year it's good and happy,
Then something bad happens.

Stephanie Johnson (10)
St Mary's RC School, Malton

GHOSTS

I'd like to be a ghost
(for being a ghost is cool)
and ghosts can play all day they don't even go to
school.

I wish I could be a ghost
to trick all my friends.
But wait a minute . . . I wouldn't have any friends.

Sean Quinn (8)
St Mary's RC School, Malton

MY WAY THROUGH THE WOODS

I started my way through
The woods when I was 13,
I went as a dare, but as I became
Frightened, the animals gave me courage
To move on, over the slippery, slimy mud.
As I feel the bushes brush against me and the
Leaves constantly rustling, the rabbits
Running into burrows as winter creeps up.
When night
Falls on the
Old dim wood
And rain makes
Ripples on the
Lake, the frogs
Leap on by me
For a hundred
Years now gone,
Owls swoop from
Tree to tree to rest
Up on a branch, I
Walk by the prickly
Bushes, the mud squelches
Between my ghostly toes, I died
20 years ago but my soul still goes
On through the never-ending woods.

Natalie Rookes (10)
St Mary's RC School, Malton

THE SPIDER

He dozes dreamily at the door.
He slips slowly and silently to the stair.
He walks wearily but willingly up the wall.
He creeps and crawls across the ceiling
To weave his web in a corner.

Elizabeth Harvey (9)
St Mary's RC School, Malton

UP, UP AND AWAY

I wish I could fly in a rocket so high instead of being in school.
To go and see Mars,
Aliens so large,
So high in the stars,
Look there's Saturn
With a ring round its belly,
A little higher there's the Sun
With flaming hair
Waving around light.

Danielle Graham (8)
Snape County Primary School

BIRDS

The birds are flying like the wind,
In and out of the trees they go.

Looping the loop, looping the loop,
Looping the loop, looping the loop.

Making patterns in the sky,
I like the birds.

Rebecca Djoric (7)
Snape County Primary School

SCREACH THE EAGLE

My friend Screach the eagle
Flies like an aeroplane,
Does tricks like a rollercoaster,
Twisting and turning,
Looping the loop,
Having fun!

James Deal (8)
Snape County Primary School

SPACE

Up in the stars,
There's Mars,
There's Mercury,
There's Saturn,
With a huge ring around,
Orange with bumps.
There's the Sun,
There's Pluto,
There's Venus,
Boiling hot,
Showing the way.

Charlotte Deal (8)
Snape County Primary School

UP, UP AND AWAY

Sometimes when I look up at the sky,
I feel like flying up, up and away,
Right up to that clear blue blanket,
I'd look down at great mountains and seas,
I'd look up at those golden rays and think of laughter.
I know how happy I would feel,
I would feel proud to drift on a cloud.
I just want to escape.

Imogen Brown (9)
Snape County Primary School

FLYING LESSONS

When I went for flying lessons,
Everything went wrong.
First I tried balloons,
And I flew into a tree,
Then I thought, why me!

Second, I tried a propeller,
Everything was perfect!
Until . . .
A Big,
Long,
Fat aeroplane crashed into me,
And I was seeing stars!

That gave me my idea
For my next extravaganza,
Wings!
I made them,
Yes!
They were excellent!
I was soaring in the air.

Shouting *Whoopee!*
And then I plunged Down
                Down
                    Down
To the ground.
I was in hospital for six weeks!

Then I thought I wouldn't fly,
I am fine as I am.

David Sharpe (9)
Snape County Primary School

READY OR NOT

What shall we play?
I don't know!
I know! *Tig!*
Nah! That's boring,
Hide and seek. Yes! I count, you hide. O.K!

Go on then. Hide!
1,2,3 they've gone a long way.
4,5,6 I'm still counting,
7,8,9 not far to go.
10,11,12 Helen's trainers are squeaking.
13,14,15 I can hear Tessa giggling,
16,17,18 somebody coughed.
19,20 here I come, ready or not!

Where are you?
Are you in the bush?
No! Are you behind the wall?
No! Are you in the playhouse?
No! Are you behind the car?
No! Where are you?
I know where you are! In the shed. No!

How did you get there?

Colette Cowley (9)
Spennithorne CE Primary School

SEASONS

Spring is when the little birds sing
And new grown flowers come out to play
The fresh dew sparkles on new green grass
It makes me happy as I pass.

Summer brings the warm sunshine
Children laughing all the time
Bucket and spade and ice-cream weather
See lots of families get together.

Autumn, looks like summer's gone away
Children gone indoors to play
Leaves gone red, yellow and brown
Like a sheet upon the ground.

Winter is here all chilly and white
Gives the animals quite a fright
Snowmen dancing, children screaming
Mums and Dads glowing and beaming.

All the seasons have passed by
Spring, summer, autumn, winter
Around they go every year
Not changing not one little bit . . .

Helen Graham (10)
Spennithorne CE Primary School

TREES AND SEASONS

Trunks, leaves, branches, trees,
Scaly, crunched, crinkled, rough.
The tree does its best to support
All of the tree.

Buds opening, small leaves appearing,
Sunlight filtering through the green
Above our head.
Long awaited, spring has arrived.

Full bloom, leafy-green ceiling,
Shades out the bright light,
All shades of green are above,
Wonderful summer is here now,
Long may it last.

Dark greens, light greens, oranges,
Reds, browns and yellows,
This time of the year is the
Season of autumn.

Dark, dull, leaves all gone now,
Branches all sparkly covered in
Frost,
Here is winter, cold and white.

Sarah Reed (10)
Spennithorne CE Primary School

PET DAY

It was National Pet Day,
The headmaster was sad,
The pets were going crazy,
The teachers were going mad.

Henry had his dog,
Jenny had her cat,
Johnny had his bird,
Carol had her rat.

Henry's dog barked madly,
Carol's rat got free,
Johnny's bird squawked hour after hour,
Jenny's cat saw the rat and thought of tea.

The judges hadn't come yet,
So the headmaster sat scratching his scalp,
He knew that no judges, no prizes,
Then the teachers would pull their hair out.

It was National Pet Day,
The judges hadn't come,
The teachers were relieved,
As children and pets went home.

Laura Laycock (11)
Sutton-In-Craven CP School

ALONE AT HOME

Suddenly there's a knock at the door,
Mum's at the shop,
What do I do,
Do I answer?
Do I dare?
Or shall I sit
And wait there.

The room is pitch-black (I mean pitch-black),
The clock's ticking,
I want my mum.
In my big street,
No one's home,
I want my mum.
I'm alone.

I turn on the TV when I'm scared,
I turn it up,
Wait, is that mum?
The car pulls up,
Mum is home,
The door opens
I'm not alone.

Jennifer Vincent (11)
Sutton-In-Craven CP School

MY IMAGINATION

Frankenstein is coming, he's at the front door,
There's a werewolf in our garden ready for a war.
There's banging in the attic, what could it be?
I think it's a zombie, that's going to get me.

The mummy's in his tomb,
There's something in my room,
I wake up with a scream,
Because I have had a bad dream.

Joe Page (11)
Sutton-In-Craven CP School

FOOTBALL

Football is great,
Football is fun,
I support a team,
Who is at the top
Of the league.

I have a dream team
But I can't say
Their names,
Some Man U, Leeds
and City.

I love footy,
I play it all the time,
It's great,
It's great,
I can't stop to play.

Jamie Lang (10)
Sutton-In-Craven CP School

THE SPITFIRE

I am the Spitfire,
Licensed to kill,
I fire at the Germans,
I fire at will.

I'm armed with eight deadly machine guns,
They're mounted under each wing,
When I let them loose,
They don't half sing.

I'm coloured with khaki,
With the RAF badge,
I'm distinct from the Germans,
But just by a tadge.

Mark Blackie (10)
Sutton-In-Craven CP School

2000

The year 2000's the year that will count,
So join with the world and come on let's shout.
Let's wipe out hunger, starvation and war,
Come on everyone, let's abide by God's law.
No more poverty, debts or abuse, ·
Let's all give God's world a better use.
We'll erase cruelty, violence and hate,
Let's save God's world from a dreadful fate.
The year 2000's the year that will count,
So join with the world and come on let's shout!

Simon Hunter (11)
Sutton-In-Craven CP School

WHO AM I?

I can be her in the day,
But I can pass quietly away,
I can travel faster than sound,
But I'm much quieter than a hound.
I can fly through the sky,
And I can pass quietly by.
My friend is thunder,
But he's quite a blunder.
I can bring clouds that cover the sun,
I think it's fun.
                    Who Am I?

Vicky Wilcock (11)
Sutton-In-Craven CP School

I BELIEVE

I believe in magic, in fairies and in trolls,
I believe in Dracula, Nessie and live dolls,
I believe in mermaids with long, flowing hair,
I believe in Pooh bear being a real live bear,
I believe that someone will lead this world to peace,
I believe that no one will ever act like geese,
I believe that politicians will finally say the truth,
I believe that I will never lose another tooth,
I believe that in the future that the world will be perfect,
I believe that never again will people be in debt.

Stephanie Boyle (11)
Sutton-In-Craven CP School

BRUCE

'Bruce, Bruce' calls mother,
To my naughty little brother,
Cos he's ripped his new shirt,
And got covered in dirt.

'Shout, shout' goes mother,
At my naughty little brother,
Cos he's coloured on his wallpaper,
And screwed up all my brand-
New paper.

'Snore, snore' goes my brother,
'Phew, phew' goes mother,
Cos my little brother's fast
Asleep in bed,
The little sleepy-head.

Shelley Williams (11)
Sutton-In-Craven CP School

MESSY BEDROOM

Mini CD player (no batteries),
Eraser (half rubbed out),
School work (behind the door),
Socks (none with a pair),
Yo-yo (unravelled),
Bed sheets (off bed),
Elastic band (snapped),
Door (wide open),
Rubbish (everywhere),
Ornaments (off shelf),
Orange peel (hidden),
Must tidy up.

Christina Longbottom (10)
Sutton-In-Craven CP School

THE FIGHT

Twelve boys in a big ring,
Two lads having a fight within.
One is doing well, the other is on the floor,
Then supergrass Sam walks through the
School door.

But Sam quickly turns around,
Then all is silent until the dreaded sound
Of footsteps announcing Miss Brown,
She quickly pulls one boy from the ground.

She shouted *'Who started this?'*
They all looked blank except for Chris
Who raised his fat hand in the air
And answered 'It was him Miss, over there!'

Thomas Clarkson (10)
Sutton-In-Craven CP School

IF I COULD DRIVE

If I could drive a car
I would drive it very far
I wouldn't care who I saw
I wouldn't knock on any doors
I'd look at the sky,
I'd look at the sea,
Then rush back home for my tea.

Emma Longbottom (10)
Sutton-In-Craven CP School

I'D LIKE TO BE A . . .

I'd like to be a shark tamer,
I'd like to be a baby namer,
I'd like to be a superstar,
I'd like to drive a sporty car.

I'd like to be a newsreader,
I'd like to be a great leader,
I'd like to grow exotic plants,
I'd like to go to other lands.

I'd like to dive under the sea,
I'd like to set prisoners free,
I'd like to be in my own Heaven,
It's a shame I'm only eleven.

Emily Jenkins (11)
Sutton-In-Craven CP School

TIGER

Crawling through the long, green grass,
Getting ready to pounce on an animal,
He goes creeping through the jungle,
Scaring all the animals,
This animal is a *tiger!*
The tiger is a very fierce animal,
Who strolls around the jungle,
Like he owns the place.

Jennifer Lorimer (10)
Sutton-In-Craven CP School

MY SCHOOL

Mrs Pendle and Miller,
Teach like a filler,
Reception and Yr 1 are quite good,
They really stay away from the mud.

Mr Wright teaches Yr 2,
There's only really a few,
They like to learn,
In P.E, they like to turn.

Miss Vernon has Yr 3,
They all love to see,
How teachers love to learn,
About a Greek urn.

Miss Gedge has Yr 4,
They ask for quite more,
The Portacabin they're in,
It's packed like a tin.

Mrs Atkinson, I like,
She teaches us alike,
Yr 5 we are,
We once drew a car.

Yr 6 are glad,
They have a lad,
Mr Gibson he's called,
To him we applaud.

Mrs Rayment our head,
She always said,
'Be good,
For fear of the wood.'

Olivia Tinker (10)
Tadcaster East Community Primary School

THE PEACEFUL FOREST

I walked through the wood,
I wanted to stroke the deer, but didn't know if I should.
The atmosphere was ghostly,
It was as if I was being watched.
I listened for a moment, then carried on
Creeping slowly, I looked around myself
So quiet was the wood, it was as if it had been cursed.

The creaking leaves
And the trickling water in the stream
The clean water everybody needs
And the little plants growing like a team
The rabbits all have habits
The deer always rears
The fox curls up like a cardboard box
The badgers are in night-time bright,
Chirp, chirp, chirp says a bird
Ekk, ekk, ekk said an owl
The wolf let out a great howl
My mother always said the birds were in herds!

The forest, so wild
I imagined a ghost jumping out to say *Boo!* But it didn't.
The forest was quiet as usual, it always had been and it
Always will.

It used to be a wacky place
Where people used to climb trees
And kick leaves
They used to swing in trees and swing in various places
And the little bench where people tied their shoe laces.

It's stopped being wacky now
'It's lonely', I say
The big bully used to say
The ghost is watching you right now
So now, nobody comes.

Emma Carr (9)
Tadcaster East Community Primary School

ABOUT A FOOTBALL MATCH

We had a game of football,
It hit me on my head,
It went straight in the net,
Jamie scored in the last minute.
   Second-half
In the first minute I scored my second goal,
Then I scored my hat-trick then the score was 6-0,
Josh has just scored and 7-1 to us.

We had a game of football,
It hit me on my leg,
It hit him straight on his head,
Then I scored my second goal straight
In the net,
Then Jamie scored a goal straight in
The net.
   Full Time.

Ben Gilmore (10)
Tadcaster East Community Primary School

MILLENNIUM PARTY

Looking in the wardrobe,
What shall I wear,
Shall I wear this, I'm going spare.

A long windy limo,
Half the road filled,
We're here at the party place,
Like cat and dog to the party
We chase.

Music banging in our ears,
Party poppers pop all year,
Fireworks flash, bright colours,
Finishing for this year.

Lucy Allison (9)
Tadcaster East Community Primary School

I WENT TO GET A BRACE

I wasn't going to school today
I was going to the dreaded place,
To the *dentist* for a *brace.*

I was getting on my parents' nerves,
Asking all these questions
About whether it hurt.

My dad said 'They say
You need false teeth after that',
My mum said 'If you listen to your dad,
You wouldn't want to go'.

Good job I listened to Mum.

Catherine Tillett (10)
Tadcaster East Community Primary School

The Big, Hungry Fox

The big, hungry fox pounced on top of the rock
That was right by the trickling river,
Then all of a sudden, out popped a small fish,
Who was suddenly starting to shiver.
'What's the matter, my friend?'
Asked the cunning fox, with a hint of slyness and glee,
Then the fox made a grab for the miniature fish,
But it squirmed and wriggled free.

So, the fox trotted off to another place -
Deep down in the murky woods,
Looking for something good to eat
Which to his surprise, he could.
Up in the high skyscraper trees
Sat a plump, ebony crow,
'He's perfect!' Hissed the greedy fox,
But as he climbed up, he broke his toe.

By the end, the poor thin fox
Was starving to death and weak,
So all the animals of the wood
Gave him a year's supply of leeks.

Pamela Bustard (11)
Thirsk CP School

NIGHT

Wolves are howling,
Cats are prowling,
But the moon keeps on watching.

Dogs are sleeping,
Mice are squeaking,
But the stars keep on shining.

Owls are hunting,
Pigs are grunting,
But the planets keep on spinning.

The birds are singing,
The frost is showing,
As the darkness starts to fade
To let the sun take over,
Until the moon with the stars
And the stars with the planets,
Come again,
To be recognised
In the dark, ebony night sky.

Hannah Bryan (10)
Thirsk CP School

TEMPTATION

Chocolate, chocolate, everywhere,
In my mouth a sticky eclair.

Chocolate, chocolate everywhere,
Even in the old man's hair.

Chocolate puddings,
Chocolate cakes,
Even yummy After Eights.

Chocolate nuts,
Chocolate flakes,
Chocolate teddies,
Chocolate snakes.

Chocolate castles,
Chocolate pigs,
Chocolate houses and chocolate drinks,
Chocolate everywhere *me thinks!*

Megan Choules (10)
Thirsk CP School

THE MOON

The moon is a guardian spreading its glow,
Attacking the darkness with its army of stars,
Showing its glistening armour with leopard-like pride.
Its gleam is an intimidating sight,
Like a thousand of Heaven's angels grouping into a ball.

The darkness draws monsters in the black night sky,
But the moon attacks with a lion's ferocity,
Scattering the dark like a hunter does to oxen.
The moon's job is done,
It has destroyed the darkness,
It marches away with its army of stars,
As the sun fixes itself in the sky,
Like a nail to wood,
Only to recall the moon to beat out the darkness again.

Christopher Hume (10)
Thirsk CP School

ONCE I SAW . . .

Once I saw a funny sight,
I saw it then, that very night.
A cat and mouse I swear I saw,
Were standing there paw in paw.
What a peculiar sight to see,
I bet no one saw it, except me.
All alone I stood, but then,
I truly thought I'd heard some men.
I went towards it, till I saw,
Them standing there paw in paw.
I ran away, I ran straight home,
I ran straight past the Millennium Dome.
I never saw them there again,
What a pity, what a pain!
And so my adventure ended,
And mice never again defended,
From mean and horrible cats,
That went around just killing rats.

Samantha Bell (9)
Topcliffe CE School

THE SQUIRREL IN THE GARDEN

Out of my bedroom window
I look into the garden
And I see the squirrel up the tree.
It stares and looks at me.

I look into the garden
I see it on the ground.
The squirrel's tail is curved and flicked.
All of a sudden it disappears.

Imogen Shaw (8)
Topcliffe CE School

WISH, WISH, WISH

I wish I was good at football
I wish I could play for Man United
My favourite player is David Beckham
I've always wanted to play mid-field.

I wish I could be a boxer
I wish I had a brother
I wish I was rich
I wish I had a swimming pool.

I wish I had a dog
I wish I lived in a palace
I wish I had a sports car
I wish the world was made of sweets.

I wish there was no such thing as school
I wish I could fly
I wish I went to bed at midnight
I wish I was an artist.

Liam Tinkler (8)
Topcliffe CE School

WISH, WISH, WISH

I wish nobody would call me names.
I wish I had a swimming pool.
I wish I was not a pain.
I wish I saw a mole.
I wish I could read and write properly.
I wish I was good at school.
I wish I could walk on the moon.
I wish my sister was not a pain.
I wish I would grow up soon.
I wish I could run down the lane.

Robert Turner (8)
Topcliffe CE School

ON THE WAY TO SWIMMING

Chairs clattering
Everyone pushing
Bags are grabbed
Footsteps walking
Children queuing silently
Bus arriving
Seatbelt clicking
Journey starting
Cars zooming
Brakes squeaking
Now it is time for splashing.

Vincent Mayville (8)
Topcliffe CE School

CUSTOMERS, BEWARE!

The manager grinned from ear to ear
As he discussed his plan,
'This'll bring more customers,'
Said the crafty man.

'People will come by the hundreds
Spending loads of cash,
And I will open,' He declared,
'The dodgy sale bash!'

He continued 'From half-price
To buy one, get one free,
Everything will be on sale
As far as eyes can see!'

But customers, be careful,
Don't let your mind run wild,
You could spend a fortune,
And make the manager smile.

If you go into his shop,
Customer, beware!
Be careful what you spend
Or even just don't go in there!

Jonathan Mozley (10)
Topcliffe CE School

WISH, WISH, WISH

I wish I had three cats.
I wish I could see whales.
I wish I had a pet bat.
I wish my mum could play the scales.

I wish my dad had a posh car.
I wish I could see air.
I wish my mum ran a bar.
I wish I had a hare.

I wish nobody would die.
I wish I owned a park.
I wish nobody would lie.
I wish there wasn't any dark.

I wish we had a swimming pool.
I wish I could wear high-heeled boots.
I wish I was cool.
I wish I liked lots of fruits.

Chloe Mathews (8)
Topcliffe CE School